11+ Verbal Activity

Cloze Tests

TESTBOOK 1

Dr Stephen C Curran
with Warren Vokes

Edited by Katrina MacKay & Andrea Richardson

This book belongs to

Accelerated Education Publications Ltd.

Guidance Notes for Parents

Cloze procedure involves supplying missing words or parts of words that have been deleted from a portion of text. Cloze tests require the ability to understand context and vocabulary in order to identify the correct words or parts of words that belong in the deleted passages of text.

Cloze passages include various forms of text:
- **Historical**
- **Biographical**
- **General Knowledge**
- **Literary Text - Prose**
- **Literary Text - Poetry**

There are three question types:

- **Missing Letters**
  In Missing Letters style questions the Cloze passage has a number of words where letters have to be provided to complete the word.

- **Multiple-choice**
  In Multiple-choice style questions there are three alternatives for the missing word in the Cloze passage.

- **Word Bank**
  In Word Bank style questions there are a number of alternatives provided in a set of words at the top of the page. Words are chosen from this Word Bank to fill the spaces in the Cloze passage.

Marking and Feedback
- The answers are provided at the back of this book.
- Only these answers are allowed.
- One mark should be given for each correct answer.
- Do not deduct marks for wrong answers.
- Do not allow half marks or 'the benefit of the doubt', as this might mask a child's need for extra help in the topic.
- Always try to be positive and encouraging.
- Talk through any mistakes with your child and work out together how to arrive at the right answer, using a dictionary if necessary.

Cloze Test 1

Choose the correct words from the word bank below to complete the passage.

spume	running	sweet	vagrant	denied
laughing	flung	shaking	whetted	windy

I must go down to the seas again, to the lonely sea and the sky,

And all I ask is a tall ship and a star to steer her by;

And the wheel's kick and the wind's song and the white sail's **1)** _____ ,

And a grey mist on the sea's face, and a grey dawn breaking.

I must go down to the seas again, for the call of the **2)** _____ tide

Is a wild call and a clear call that may not be **3)** _____ ;

And all I ask is a **4)** _____ day with the white clouds flying,

And the **5)** _____ spray and the blown **6)** _____ , and the

sea-gulls crying.

I must go down to the seas again, to the **7)** _____ gypsy life,

To the gull's way and the whale's way where the wind's like a

8) _____ knife;

And all I ask is a merry yarn from a **9)** _____ fellow-rover,

And quiet sleep and a **10)** _____ dream when the long trick's over.

Sea Fever by John Masefield (1878-1967).

Score _____ Percentage _____ %

Cloze Test 2

Fill in the missing letters to complete the passage below.

George Armstrong Custer was born in New Rumley, Ohio in 1839. His father was a farmer and blacksmith. He was 1) [a d m _ t _ _ d] to West Point in 1858 but, despite his longing to climb to a higher rank in life, an element of 2) [r _ b e _ l i _ n] ran through the young officer. He 3) [b u _ k l _ d] under authority, and his infractions led him to famously graduate bottom of his class.

He 4) [_ e r v _ d] with the Union Army in the American Civil War. Custer proved to be a highly 5) [e _ f e c _ i v _] cavalry commander and gained a strong reputation during the Civil War. His career was 6) [b o o _ t _ d] considerably by his association with several important officers and, in 1863, Custer was 7) [_ r o m _ t e _] from captain to brevet brigadier general of volunteers. The press often 8) [r e _ e r _ _ d] to Custer as "The Boy General", reflecting his promotion to brigadier general at the age of 23.

He and his troops played a 9) [d _ c i s _ v _] role in defeating the Confederate Army in the Appomattox 10) [_ a m p _ _ g n] and Custer was present when the commander of the Confederate Army, General Robert E. Lee, 11) [s u r _ e _ d _ r e _] to Union General Grant in 1865.

After the Civil War, Custer was **12)** | d | | s | p | | t | c | | e | d | to the west to fight in the American Indian Wars. In 1876, Custer and all the men with him were killed fighting against a **13)** | c | o | a | l | | t | | | n | of Native American tribes at the Battle of the Little Bighorn. This battle has come to be popularly known as "Custer's Last Stand."

14) | U | | f | o | | t | u | n | | t | e | | y |, the decisive **15)** | d | e | | | | t | he suffered in the Battle of the Little Bighorn has **16)** | o | | e | r | s | | a | d | o | | e | all Custer's prior achievements.

However, after his death, Custer achieved the lasting **17)** | f | | | e | that he had sought on the battlefield. The public saw him as a tragic military hero and an **18)** | e | | e | m | p | | a | r | | gentleman who **19)** | s | | c | r | i | | | c | e | d | his life for his country. Custer's wife, Elizabeth, who had accompanied him in many of his frontier expeditions, did much to **20)** | | d | v | | n | c | | this view with the publication of several books about her late husband.

Custer was buried with full military honors at West Point Cemetery in 1877.

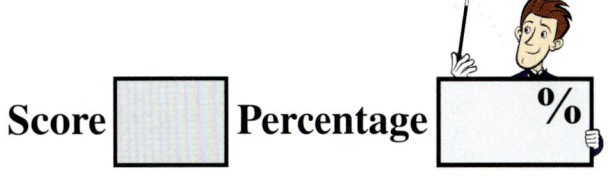

Score [ ] Percentage [ ] %

Cloze Test 3

Choose the correct words from the word bank below to complete the passage.

| motors | burning | smoke | mighty | screaming |
| recorded | slacked | horror | dropped | massive |

The Hindenburg was the largest airship ever built; over 800 feet long from its nose to its **1)** _____ tail fins. But in the space of 37 seconds this **2)** _____ zeppelin was destroyed in a fire that killed a third of its crew and passengers and left spectators crying in **3)** _____ .

A radio reporter named Herbert Morrison was covering the airship's arrival and his comments were **4)** _____ for posterity:

"... It's practically standing still now. They've **5)** _____ ropes out of the nose of the ship, and it's been taken a hold of down on the field by a number of men. It's starting to rain again; the rain had **6)** _____ up a little bit. The back **7)** _____ of the ship are just holding it, just enough to keep it from ..."

"It burst into flames! ... It's fire and it's crashing! It's crashing terrible! Oh, my! Get out of the way, please! It's **8)** _____ , bursting into flames and is falling on the mooring mast, and all the folks agree that this is terrible. This is the worst of the worst catastrophes in the world! ... There's **9)** _____ , and there's flames, now, and the frame is crashing to the ground, not quite to the mooring mast ... Oh, the humanity, and all the passengers **10)** _____ around here!"

Score ☐ Percentage ☐ %

Cloze Test 4

Select the correct words to complete the passage below.

The *Sputnik* rocket was 1) [launched / built / conceived] on 5th October 1957. The satellite separated from the rocket and its 2) [lighting / radar / transmitter] was activated and the "beep-beep-beep" tones confirmed the satellite's 3) [successful / terminal / partial] deployment. When the Soviets began using *Sputnik* in their 4) [experiments / country / propaganda], they emphasised their pride in the achievement of Soviet technology, arguing that it 5) [hampered / demonstrated / underestimated] the Soviets' superiority over the West. In Britain, the media and population 6) [later / finally / initially] reacted with a mixture of fear for the future but also amazement about mankind's 7) [reticence / boldness / progress]. Many newspapers and magazines 8) [heralded / predicted / scorned] the arrival of the space age. However, when the Soviet Union launched a second craft containing the dog, Laika, the media 9) [narrative / pressure / fears] returned to one of anti-communism and many people sent 10) [donations / protests / animals] to the Russian embassy.

Score ☐ Percentage ☐ %

Cloze Test 5

Fill in the missing letters to complete the passage below.

The word Blitz is short for Blitzkrieg, which means lightning war.

From September 1940, Britain was subjected to a night-time bombing campaign 1) **conceived** by Hitler to destroy Britain's 2) **morale**. To instil more fear into the population, the bombing raids were carried out at night. By the time it had 3) **ceased** in May 1941, in nine months the Blitz had killed 43,000 across Britain and made 1.4 million 4) **homeless**.

London was the target for the most bombing raids but Manchester, Liverpool and Glasgow were also 5) **attacked**, with Coventry and Bristol suffering extremely heavy 6) **bombardment**.

Anderson shelters, designed to 7) **accommodate** six people, were 8) **issued** by the government. The Anderson shelter was designed in 1938 and named after Sir John Anderson, the man 9) **responsible** for preparing Britain to 10) **withstand** German air raids.

However, when the air raid 11) **sirens** sounded, thousands of families 12) **descended** into London's underground stations to seek shelter from the highly **13)** e _ p l _ _ i v e and incendiary bombs. Although, at the outset, the government did not allow the use of tube stations, crowds broke through the locked and chained **14)** _ n t _ a n c _ s .

Sadly, **15)** s _ e l _ e r _ _ g in underground stations did not always **16)** p r _ v _ d _ safety. When a bomb smashed through the road above and fell into it, over 200 people were killed in the City tube station.

German pilots used the river Thames to help them **17)** _ a v i _ a t _ to London. The first wave of enemy planes flew over London and dropped **18)** _ n c _ n _ i _ r y bombs. The fires acted as a **19)** m a _ k _ r for the next wave of planes that dropped highly explosive bombs. At that time, Britain had no night-time fighters but the bombers had to cope with Anti-aircraft gun fire and **20)** a v _ _ d i _ g barrage balloons and searchlights.

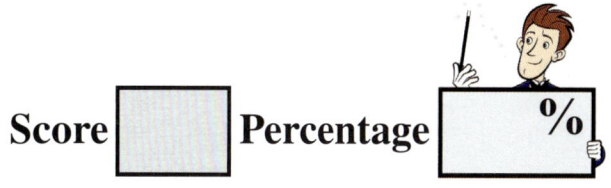

Cloze Test 6

Select the correct words to complete the passage below.

On 15th June 1215, King John **1)** [ ] renounced / [ ] issued / [ ] printed the Magna Carta (Latin: "the Great Charter") at Runnymede, near Windsor. Its purpose was to **2)** [ ] alienate / [ ] reward / [ ] reconcile the unpopular King and a group of **3)** [ ] rebel / [ ] amiable / [ ] wealth barons. It promised protection for the barons from illegal imprisonment, access to **4)** [ ] wilfull / [ ] biased / [ ] swift justice, protection of church rights and limitations on feudal **5)** [ ] payments / [ ] ties / [ ] customs to the Crown. Over 800 years old, Magna Carta still forms an important symbol of **6)** [ ] law / [ ] history / [ ] liberty today.

Legal principles, such as *habeas corpus*, are often **7)** [ ] cited / [ ] remembered / [ ] rejected by politicians and campaigners. It has been described as "the greatest **8)** [ ] constitutional / [ ] decorated / [ ] statutory document of all times – the **9)** [ ] end / [ ] fountain / [ ] foundation of the freedom of the individual against the **10)** [ ] arbitrary / [ ] ardent / [ ] lesser authority of the despot".

Score [ ]   Percentage [%]

Cloze Test 7

Choose the correct words from the word bank below to complete the passage.

betrays	tinkling	tingling	insidious	remembrance
singing	glamour	poised	manhood	vista

Softly, in the dusk, a woman is **1)** _____ to me;

Taking me back down the **2)** _____ of years, till I see

A child sitting under the piano, in the boom of the **3)** _____ strings

And pressing the small, **4)** _____ feet of a mother who smiles as she sings.

In spite of myself, the **5)** _____ mastery of song

6) _____ me back, till the heart of me weeps to belong

To the old Sunday evenings at home, with winter outside

And hymns in the cosy parlour, the **7)** _____ piano our guide.

So now it is vain for the singer to burst into clamour

With the great black piano appassionato. The **8)** _____

Of childish days is upon me, my **9)** _____ is cast

Down in the flood of **10)** _____ , I weep like a child for the past.

Piano by DH Lawrence (1885-1930).

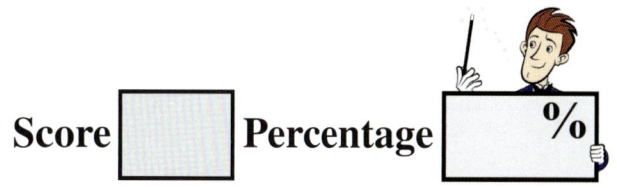

Score ☐ Percentage ☐ %

Cloze Test 8

Fill in the missing letters to complete the passage below.

The 1) **Russian** gentleman was better the next day, and the day after that better still, and on the third day he was well enough to come into the garden. A 2) **basket** chair was put for him and he sat there, dressed in clothes of Father's which were too big for him. But when Mother had 3) **hemmed** up the ends of the sleeves and the trousers, the clothes did well enough. His was a kind face now that it was no longer tired and 4) **frightened**, and he smiled at the children 5) **whenever** he saw them. They wished very much that he could speak English. Mother wrote 6) **several** letters to people she thought might know 7) **whereabouts** in England a Russian gentleman's wife and family might possibly be; not to the people she used to know before she came to live at Three Chimneys—she never wrote to any of them—but 8) **strange** people—Members of 9) **Parliament** and Editors of papers, and Secretaries of Societies.

And she did not do much of her story-writing, only 10) **corrected** proofs as she sat in the sun near the Russian, and talked to him every now and then.

The children wanted very much to show how **11)** | k | i | | | l | y | they felt to this man who had been sent to prison and to Siberia just for writing a beautiful book about poor people. They could smile at him, of course; they could and they did. But if you smile too **12)** | c | | n | | t | a | n | | l | y |, the smile is apt to get fixed like the smile of the **13)** | h | | e | n | |. And then it no longer looks friendly, but simply silly. So they tried other ways, and brought him flowers till the place where he sat was **14)** | s | | r | r | o | | n | | e | d | by little fading bunches of **15)** | c | l | | v | | r | and roses and Canterbury bells.

And then Phyllis had an idea. She **16)** | b | e | | k | o | | e | d | mysteriously to the others and drew them into the back yard, and there, in a **17)** | | o | n | c | | a | | e | d | spot, between the pump and the water-butt, she said:—

"You remember Perks **18)** | p | r | o | | i | | i | n | | me the very first strawberries out of his own garden?" Perks, you will **19)** | | | c | o | l | | e | c | t |, was the Porter. "Well, I should think they're **20)** | r | i | | | now. Let's go down and see."

Extract from *The Railway Children* by E Nesbit (1858-1924).

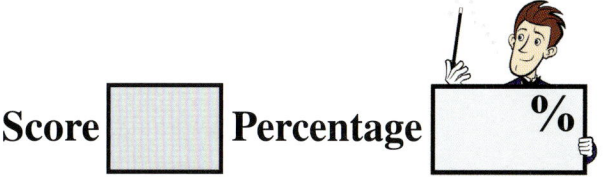

Cloze Test 9

Choose the correct words from the word bank below to complete the passage.

| coined | diet | receive | element | engrossed |
| née | native | illness | degree | radioactive |

Marie Curie 1) _____ Sklodowska was born in Warsaw, Poland on 7th November 1867. Both her parents were maths teachers and she was the youngest of five children.

In 1891 she arrived in Paris and enrolled at the Sorbonne. She was totally dedicated and 2) _____ in her studies but, with little money, she survived mainly on buttered bread and tea. Her health suffered as a result of her poor 3) _____ . She completed her master's 4) _____ in Physics in 1893 and another degree in Mathematics a year later.

A colleague introduced Marie to her future husband, the French physicist, Pierre Curie. Pierre helped Marie with her exploration of radioactivity. They worked with pitchblende and discovered a new radioactive 5) _____ in 1898. They named the element polonium, after Marie's 6) _____ country of Poland. They also detected the presence of another 7) _____ material in the pitchblende, and called that radium. Marie herself 8) _____ the word 'radioactivity'.

Marie Curie was the first woman to 9) _____ a Nobel Prize. In fact she won two: one for Chemistry and the other for Physics. Mme. Curie died in Savoy, France after a short 10) _____ in 1934.

Score ____ Percentage ____ %

Cloze Test 10

Select the correct words to complete the passage below.

Around 1435-40, Johann Gutenberg **1)** [ ] discovered / [ ] instilled / [ ] invented movable, interchangeable, reuseable type, **2)** [ ] casting / [ ] making / [ ] using metal from a reverse impression. The moulds may have been made from sand or plaster. He used a wooden **3)** [ ] spoon / [ ] stakes / [ ] press , similar to those used at the time for wine or cheese making, and his own **4)** [ ] composition / [ ] supply / [ ] container of an oily, varnish-like ink made of soot, turpentine and walnut oil. He was a silversmith by **5)** [ ] day / [ ] profession / [ ] night and used his knowledge in that field to invent the type metal alloy **6)** [ ] comprising / [ ] lacking / [ ] extruding a mixture of lead, tin and antimony. The alloy melted at a relatively **7)** [ ] high / [ ] average / [ ] low temperature for faster and more **8)** [ ] economical / [ ] colourful / [ ] technical casting. Movable type allowed a page of type to be **9)** [ ] turned / [ ] read / [ ] composed and, when no longer required, the individual **10)** [ ] characters / [ ] pages / [ ] numbers could be reused to compose a new page.

Score ____ Percentage ____ %

Cloze Test 11

Fill in the missing letters to complete the passage below.

Glaciers are formed when snowfall collects in a

1) **depression** between two mountains.

2) **Subsequent** snowfall builds up and the snow

3) **compresses** under its own weight, causing the air

4) **trapped** in the snow flakes to be

5) **expelled**. Once this happens, glacial ice is formed.

The glacial ice builds up until it 6) **overflows**

from the area where it has been trapped. This may be due to a geological

7) **weakness** or a gap between the two mountains.

The slope of the 8) **terrain**, the weight of the snow and ice, the

effects of gravity and pressure all 9) **combine** and the glacier begins

to move. As the glacier travels slowly down the valley it

10) **abrades** rock and debris from the land over which it moves.

The speed of glacial movement is 11) **typically** around a

metre per day but mean speeds vary greatly from one region to another. Where the slope

of the terrain is steeper, the ice is thicker or the snowfall

12) **increases**, speeds of 20 to 30 metres per day have been

observed.

As the glacier travels down the mountainside, landforms such as cirques and moraines are created. After a glacier has melted, **13)** l _ t e r a _ and end (or terminal) moraines may remain. These clearly indicate the **14)** w i _ t _ of the glacier and the furthest point of the glacier flow.

15) V _ s _ ice sheets in the polar regions contain almost all the glacial ice on the planet. This ice forms the largest **16)** r _ s e _ v o _ r of fresh water on Earth. However, in every continent, with the **17)** _ x c e _ t i o _ of Australia, glaciers may still be found in mountain ranges. Many of these provide melt water when the **18)** _ e m p e _ a t u _ e _ rise in the spring and summer, thus creating an often much needed water source to areas that may **19)** o t _ e r _ i s _ be **20)** l _ c _ i _ g .

Cloze Test 12

Select the correct words to complete the passage below.

It was his first 1) [ ] choice / [ ] impressions / [ ] experience of a large manufacturing city, and the crowded

tram-car with its continually 2) [ ] knocking / [ ] failing / [ ] squealing brakes frightened him. Half pushed,

half towed, he arrived at the high gate of the Kashmir Serai: that 3) [ ] huge / [ ] small / [ ] limited open

square over against the railway station, surrounded with 4) [ ] vertical / [ ] wood / [ ] arched cloisters,

where the camel and horse 5) [ ] caravans / [ ] groups / [ ] herded put up on their return from Central Asia.

Here were all manner of Northern folk, tending 6) [ ] runaway / [ ] fraction / [ ] tethered ponies and kneeling

camels; loading and unloading bales and bundles; 7) [ ] drawing / [ ] pouring / [ ] drinking water for the

evening meal at the 8) [ ] creaking / [ ] silent / [ ] rattle well-windlasses; piling grass before the shrieking,

wild-eyed stallions; 9) [ ] pat / [ ] calling / [ ] cuffing the surly caravan dogs; paying off camel-drivers;

taking on new grooms; swearing, shouting, arguing, and chaffering in the

10) [ ] packed / [ ] empty / [ ] quiet square.

Extract from *Kim*
by Rudyard Kipling (1865-1936).

Cloze Test 13

Choose the correct words from the word bank below to complete the passage.

| occurring | sedimentary | poorer | decayed | formation |
| compressed | relatively | energy | rank | primarily |

The most common source of **1)** _____ in the Western world today is oil but the second most used energy provider is still coal. Formed over 400 million years ago from the remains of dead and **2)** _____ plants such as trees and ferns, it is still mined and burnt in huge quantities.

The main types of coal are anthracite, bituminous, sub-bituminous and lignite. Anthracite is a naturally **3)** _____ smokeless fuel. It is very shiny, hard and dense and extremely slow-burning with high heat output. Bituminous coal, or black coal, is a **4)** _____ soft coal containing a tar-like substance called bitumen. It is of higher quality than lignite coal but of **5)** _____ quality than anthracite. **6)** _____ is usually the result of high pressure being exerted on lignite. Sub-bituminous coal is a type of coal, whose properties range from those of lignite to those of bituminous coal and is used **7)** _____ as fuel for steam-electric power generation. Lignite, often referred to as brown coal, is a soft brown combustible **8)** _____ rock that is formed from naturally **9)** _____ peat. It is considered the lowest **10)** _____ of coal due to its relatively low heat content.

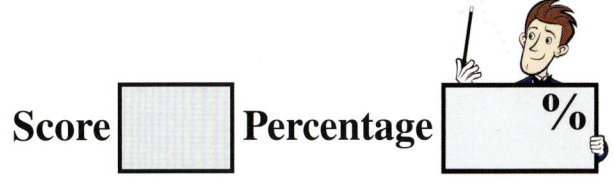

Cloze Test 14

Fill in the missing letters to complete the passage.

A boat 1) b [ ] n e a t [ ] a sunny sky,

2) L [ ] n g [ ] r i n [ ] onward dreamily

In an 3) [ ] v e n [ ] n g of July —

Children three that 4) [ ] n e [ ] t l [ ] near,

5) E [ ] g e [ ] eye and willing ear,

Pleased a 6) [ ] i m p [ ] e tale to hear —

Long has 7) p a [ ] e d that sunny sky:

8) E [ ] h o [ ] s fade and memories die:

Autumn frosts have 9) s l a [ ] n July.

Still she 10) [ ] a u n t [ ] me, phantomwise,

Alice 11) m o [ ] i n [ ] under skies

Never seen by 12) w [ ] k [ ] n g eyes.

Children yet, the **13)** | t | a | | e | to hear,

Eager eye and **14)** | | i | | l | | n | g | ear,

15) | L | o | | i | n | | l | | shall nestle near.

In a Wonderland they lie,

16) | D | | e | a | | i | | g | as the days go by,

Dreaming as the **17)** | s | | m | m | | | s | die:

Ever **18)** | d | | i | f | | i | n | | down the stream —

Lingering in the **19)** | | o | l | d | | | gleam —

Life, what is it but a **20)** | d | r | | | | ?

A Boat Beneath a Sunny Sky by Lewis Carroll (1832-1898).

Score ☐ Percentage ☐ %

Cloze Test 15

Choose the correct words from the word bank below to complete the passage.

majority	**naked**	**figure**	**iridescent**	**species**
shelter	**creatures**	**order**	**sensory**	**varieties**

Butterflies and moths both belong to the **1)** _____ Lepidoptera. *'Lepidos'* means scales and *'ptera'* means wing. There are, however, significant basic differences that separate the two **2)** _____ .

Butterflies only fly in the daytime, whereas the **3)** _____ of moths fly at night. While it is true that some moths are daytime fliers, butterflies cannot fly at night. They are solar-powered **4)** _____ and are only able to fly if their body temperature is over 30 degrees Celsius. Most butterflies will fall from the sky if they do not find **5)** _____ when the temperature drops.

The speed of flight of the slowest butterflies is five miles per hour but the fastest may reach speeds as high as thirty miles per hour. Non-poisonous butterflies are faster than the poisonous **6)** _____ . None fly in a straight line but travel in a **7)** _____ of eight pattern.

The body of a butterfly is covered entirely with tiny **8)** _____ hairs which they use while in flight to receive information about the environment and the wind. They have two pairs of large wings that are covered with **9)** _____ scales. These scales are too small to see with the **10)** _____ eye.

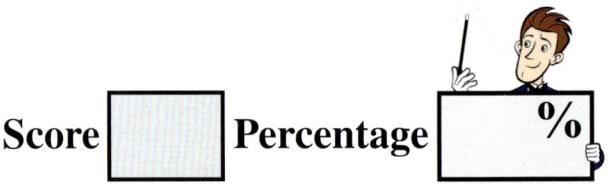

Cloze Test 16

Fill in the missing letters to complete the passage.

"Hope" is the thing with 1) f e a t h e r s -

That 2) p e r c h e s in the soul -

And sings the tune 3) w i t h o u t the words -

And never stops - at all -

And 4) s w e e t e s t - in the Gale - is heard -

And sore must be the 5) s t o r m -

That could 6) a b a s h the little Bird

That kept so many warm -

I've heard it in the 7) c h i l l i e s t land -

And on the 8) s t r a n g e s t Sea -

Yet - never - in 9) E x t r e m i t y ,

It asked a 10) c r u m b - of me.

Hope is the Thing with Feathers by Emily Dickinson (1830–1886).

Score ☐ Percentage ☐ %

Cloze Test 17

Select the correct words to complete the passage below.

On the night of which I am 1) [ ] thinking / [ ] dreaming / [ ] speaking, Stephen Elliott found himself, as he thought, looking through the 2) [ ] glazed / [ ] wooden / [ ] sturdy door. The moon was shining through the window, and he was 3) [ ] smiling / [ ] aiming / [ ] gazing at a figure which lay in the bath. His

4) [ ] vision / [ ] description / [ ] memory of what he saw reminds me of what I once beheld myself in the famous 5) [ ] vaults / [ ] staple / [ ] nave of St Michan's Church in Dublin, which possesses the

6) [ ] pleasant / [ ] horrid / [ ] torrid property of preserving corpses from 7) [ ] robbers / [ ] light / [ ] decay for centuries. A figure inexpressibly thin and pathetic, of a 8) [ ] dusty / [ ] rustic / [ ] bright leaden colour, enveloped in a shroud-like garment, the thin lips 9) [ ] crooked / [ ] purse / [ ] beaten into a faint and dreadful smile, the hands pressed 10) [ ] open / [ ] limp / [ ] tightly over the region of the heart. As he looked upon it, a distant, almost 11) [ ] inaudible / [ ] raucous / [ ] human moan seemed to issue from its lips, and the arms began to 12) [ ] sweet / [ ] melt / [ ] stir. The terror of the sight forced Stephen backwards and he

13) ☐ awoke / ☐ came / ☐ buckled to the fact that he was indeed standing on the cold

14) ☐ plank / ☐ carpeted / ☐ boarded floor of the passage in the full light of the moon. With a

15) ☐ courage / ☐ shrug / ☐ moan which I do not think can be 16) ☐ pragmatic / ☐ thoughtful / ☐ common among boys of his

age, he went to the door of the bathroom to 17) ☐ hear / ☐ ascertain / ☐ recall if the figure of his

dreams were really there. It was not, and he went back to bed. Mrs Bunch was much

18) ☐ impressed / ☐ bored / ☐ rebuffed next morning by his story, and went so far as to replace the

19) ☐ muslin / ☐ leather / ☐ wooden curtain over the glazed door of the bathroom. Mr Abney, moreover,

to whom he 20) ☐ relished / ☐ constructed / ☐ confided his experiences at breakfast, was greatly interested

and made notes of the matter in what he called 'his book'.

Extract from *The Lost Hearts* by MR James (1862-1936).

Cloze Test 18

Select the correct words to complete the passage below.

When the Panama canal lock **1)** [ ] system / [ ] gates / [ ] sluices   opened in 1914, it was one of the

greatest **2)** [ ] excavation / [ ] evacuation / [ ] engineering   works ever undertaken. There are three sets of locks,

each having two parallel **3)** [ ] flights / [ ] beams / [ ] lane , so that in principle ships may pass in

opposite directions at the same time. However, with large ships this is not possible, so

one **4)** [ ] vessel / [ ] captain / [ ] vehicle   passes through in one direction, then another moves in the

5) [ ] same / [ ] northerly / [ ] opposite   direction using the parallel chamber. The lock chambers are

6) [ ] massive / [ ] minute / [ ] meagre   and each one requires over 100,000 cubic metres of water to fill it.

Three large culverts **7)** [ ] buried / [ ] enclosed / [ ] embedded   in the walls of each chamber carry water from

the **8)** [ ] lake / [ ] mountains / [ ] well   above and then through each lock to the sea below. The lock

gates are **9)** [ ] enormous / [ ] enchanting / [ ] encrusted : each is over 2 metres thick and the **10)** [ ] tallest / [ ] oldest / [ ] heaviest

weighs over 650 tonnes.

Score [ ]   Percentage [ ] %

Cloze Test 19

Select the correct words to complete the passage below.

The English short story writer, poet and 1) [ ] novelist / [ ] hunter / [ ] journalism Joseph Rudyard Kipling

was born in Bombay in 1865. At the age of five, he was 2) [ ] carried / [ ] bought / [ ] brought to England

by his parents. Kipling wrote 3) [ ] scary / [ ] numerous / [ ] silly short stories and poems. Perhaps his

best-known children's 4) [ ] poem / [ ] choice / [ ] classic is *The Jungle Book*: a favourite among children

and made into a very popular 5) [ ] anonymous / [ ] animated / [ ] annotated film by Walt Disney Productions in

1967. In 1907, Kipling became the first English language writer to be

6) [ ] awarded / [ ] sold / [ ] awaiting the Nobel Prize in Literature and, at the age of 42, remains its

youngest 7) [ ] recreant / [ ] reward / [ ] recipient . In his lifetime he 8) [ ] declared / [ ] declined / [ ] depicted both a knighthood

and the 9) [ ] appeal / [ ] appointment / [ ] applause as British Poet Laureate. Kipling kept writing, though

with much less 10) [ ] success / [ ] succour / [ ] surplus , until the early 1930s and died in January 1936,

aged 70.

Score [   ] Percentage [   ]%

Cloze Test 20

Choose the correct words from the word bank below to complete the passage.

thatched	trunks	lashed	inhabitants	illustrations
landfall	blade	genetic	indigenous	companions
hemp	comprised	plaited	dimensions	Inca
settled	crewed	conclude	display	smashed

In 1947, the Norwegian explorer and writer, Thor Heyerdahl, set sail from South America to the Polynesian Islands. Heyerdahl believed that people from South America could have **1)** _____ Polynesia before Columbus discovered America. Most anthropologists now **2)** _____ that this was not the case but new **3)** _____ evidence does show that **4)** _____ of Easter Island do possess some South American DNA.

Kon-Tiki was the name of the raft used by Heyerdahl. It was named after the **5)** _____ sun god, Viracocha, for whom Kon-Tiki is said to be an old name. The raft **6)** _____ a float with bow splashboards and centre boards, a cabin, a mast with main sail, and a steering oar.

A small team helped Heyerdahl build the raft in Peru using native materials. Its design conformed to an **7)** _____ style that was recorded in **8)** _____ made by Spanish conquistadors.

Nine balsa tree **9)** _____ with cross pieces of balsa logs were lashed together with **10)** _____ ropes. Pine was used for the splashboards and centre boards. Lengths of mangrove wood **11)** _____ together in an A-frame provided the main mast behind which was the cabin. This was made of

12) _____ bamboo with a 13) _____ roof of banana leaves. The 9 metres long steering oar was also made from mangrove wood with a 14) _____ of fir. The overall 15) _____ of the craft were 21.25 metres long by 8.5 metres wide. The mast was nearly 14 metres high and supported a main sail that measured 7 x 8.5 metres.

The expedition, 16) _____ by Heyerdahl and five 17) _____ , set off on 28th April, 1947. They sailed for 101 days and travelled over 6,900km. Their journey ended on 7th August 1947 when Kon-Tiki 18) _____ into a reef at Raroria in the Tuamotu Islands and the crew made successful 19) _____ .

The original Kon-Tiki raft is now on 20) _____ in the Kon-Tiki Museum in Bygdøy, near Oslo.

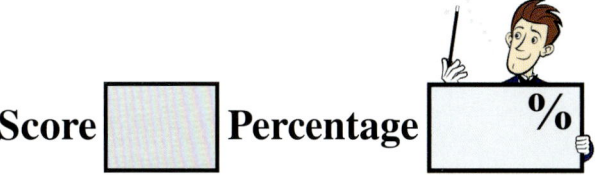

Cloze Test 21

Fill in the missing letters to complete the passage below.

The building of Hadrian's Wall began in AD 122 and was largely completed in six years. Construction 1) c_mmen__d in the east from Wallsend on the River Tyne and extended 80 Roman miles, or 117.5km (73.0 miles), to the west 2) _ermi_at_ng just west of Bowness-on-Solway on the shore of the Solway Firth. The Wall was 3) pro__ab__ planned before Hadrian's visit to Britain in AD 122 and reasons for its construction 4) __ary. There is no recording of an exact explanation but Hadrian's wish to keep "intact the empire" may have been a 5) d__mi_an_ factor in the decision to build the Wall. However, the inhabitants of northern Britain may not have 6) __os__d a significant threat and doubt has been expressed about the economic 7) a_va_ta_es of building a fixed line of defence like the Wall. Over the 8) e__su_n_ years much of the wall has disappeared. In the 18th century long sections of the Wall were removed and used to build roads to move troops to crush the Jacobean 9) i_surre_ti_n. Much of the Wall that remains owes its presence to the efforts of John Clayton, a lawyer and town clerk of Newcastle in the 1830s, who became 10) e_th_si_sti_ about the Wall's preservation. The National Trust has purchased the land on which the Wall stands and, in 1987, Hadrian's Wall was declared a World Heritage Site.

Cloze Test 22

Select the correct words to complete the passage below.

1) ☐ Science ☐ Evidence ☐ Presence | exists of the ancient Egyptians 2) ☐ forgetting ☐ practising ☐ allowing | the craft of

cheesemaking more than 5,000 years ago. It is a process that allows milk to be

3) ☐ boiled ☐ preserved ☐ eaten | whilst maintaining its nutritional and economic

4) ☐ appearance ☐ value ☐ calories | . It is likely that nomadic herdsmen stored milk in

5) ☐ bottles ☐ vessels ☐ urns | made from the stomachs of sheep and goats. Stored in this way, the

milk would 6) ☐ repulse ☐ react ☐ repeal | with the lactic acid and bacteria in the stomach lining

causing it to ferment and 7) ☐ decay ☐ coagulate ☐ escape | creating a kind of yogurt. By a process

of gentle 8) ☐ persuasion ☐ agitation ☐ stroking | , curds could be separated from whey resulting in the

production of cheese. Nowadays, a cheesemaker's 9) ☐ salary ☐ objective ☐ object | is to produce a

wide range of cheeses with specific and consistent characteristics in every

10) ☐ barrel ☐ batch ☐ dish | .

Score ☐ Percentage ☐ %

Cloze Test 23

Choose the correct words from the word bank below to complete the passage.

retreated	**sled**	**vague**	**coy**	**dubiously**
bounding	**dissipated**	**regaining**	**traces**	**corresponding**
holding	**mincing**	**menacing**	**snarl**	**cautious**
rifle	**luring**	**mistake**	**sniffed**	**ingratiating**

But One Ear broke into a run across the snow, his **1)** _____ trailing behind him. And there, out in the snow of their back track, was the she-wolf waiting for him. As he neared her, he became suddenly **2)** _____ . He slowed down to an alert and **3)** _____ walk and then stopped. He regarded her carefully and **4)** _____ , yet desirefully. She seemed to smile at him, showing her teeth in an **5)** _____ rather than a **6)** _____ way. She moved toward him a few steps, playfully, and then halted. One Ear drew near to her, still alert and cautious, his tail and ears in the air, his head held high. He tried to sniff noses with her, but she **7)** _____ playfully and coyly. Every advance on his part was accompanied by a **8)** _____ retreat on her part. Step by step she was **9)** _____ him away from the security of his human companionship. Once, as though a warning had in **10)** _____ ways flitted through his intelligence, he turned his head and looked back at the overturned sled, at his team-mates, and at the two men who were calling to him. But whatever idea was forming in his mind, was **11)** _____ by the she-wolf, who advanced upon him, **12)** _____ noses with him for a fleeting instant, and then resumed her **13)** _____ retreat before his renewed advances.

In the meantime, Bill had bethought himself of the **14)** _____ . But it was jammed beneath the overturned **15)** _____ , and by the time Henry had helped him to right the load, One Ear and the she-wolf were too close together and the distance too great to risk a shot.

Too late One Ear learned his **16)** _____ . Before they saw the cause, the two men saw him turn and start to run back toward them. Then, approaching at right angles to the trail and cutting off his retreat they saw a dozen wolves, lean and grey, **17)** _____ across the snow. On the instant, the she-wolf's coyness and playfulness disappeared. With a **18)** _____ she sprang upon One Ear. He thrust her off with his shoulder, and, his retreat cut off and still intent on **19)** _____ the sled, he altered his course in an attempt to circle around to it. More wolves were appearing every moment and joining in the chase. The she-wolf was one leap behind One Ear and **20)** _____ her own.

Extract from *White Fang* by Jack London (1876-1916).

Cloze Test 24

Fill in the missing letters to complete the passage below.

During World War II, the United Kingdom, as an island nation, was highly 1) dependent on imported goods. Germany was 2) determined to prevent merchant ships supplying Britain and her allies with the food, weapons and 3) materials that enabled them to continue fighting. Allied convoys sailed from North America destined 4) predominantly for the United Kingdom and the Soviet Union. The navies and air forces of Britain and Canada were hard pressed to give 5) protection to the Allied convoys against the threat from enemy submarines that 6) stalked the merchant vessels. Winston Churchill coined the name "Battle of the Atlantic" in February 1941. It has been called the "longest, largest, and most complex" naval battle in history. Churchill also said, "The Battle of the Atlantic was the 7) dominating factor all through the war. Never for one moment could we forget that everything happening elsewhere, on land, at sea or in the air depended 8) ultimately on its outcome." The 9) campaign started immediately after the European war began, and lasted six years. The outcome of the battle was a 10) strategic victory for the Allies.

Cloze Test 25

Select the correct words to complete the passage below.

Thomas Becket was born around 1120AD. He 1) ☐ achieved ☐ attended ☐ resisted grammar school and, when his father's fortunes 2) ☐ improved ☐ blossomed ☐ declined, Thomas was forced to seek employment as a clerk. He later 3) ☐ acquired ☐ admired ☐ amassed a position in the household of Theobald of Bec, the Archbishop of Canterbury. Thomas was sent on several 4) ☐ ships ☐ missions ☐ missives to Rome and educated in canon law. In 1154 he was 5) ☐ named ☐ given ☐ denied Archdeacon of Canterbury and became Lord Chancellor to Henry II. When 6) ☐ found ☐ lost ☐ confirmed in the position of Archbishop of Canterbury in 1162, a 7) ☐ wedge ☐ rift ☐ rank grew between him and the King as Becket sought to recover and extend the rights of the archbishopric. He was 8) ☐ aware ☐ convicted ☐ convinced of contempt of royal authority and in 1170, after six years in 9) ☐ exile ☐ waiting ☐ extreme, he returned to England where he was 10) ☐ calmly ☐ briefly ☐ brutally assassinated in Canterbury Cathedral.

Score ☐   Percentage ☐ %

Cloze Test 26

Choose the correct words from the word bank below to complete the passage.

droplets	appearance	hail	gas	eventually
crystals	endless	altitude	wispy	atmosphere
obscure	identification	bubbles	varies	precipitation
process	meteorologist	shapes	cycle	condensed

The water **1)** _____ begins when water from oceans, lakes, rivers and plants evaporates in the heat of the sun. As it evaporates, it rises into the **2)** _____ as a **3)** _____ and, as it rises higher, it cools and clouds are formed. The clouds gather more and more **4)** _____ water and the **5)** _____ become larger and heavier. **6)** _____ , they become too heavy to rise further or be supported by the rising warm air. The heavy water droplets then fall as **7)** _____ . This may be in the form of rain, snow, sleet or **8)** _____ . In this way, water returns to the oceans, lakes and soil for the **9)** _____ to continue in an **10)** _____ cycle.

The shape and appearance of clouds **11)** _____ . In 1803 Luke Howard, a pharmacist and amateur **12)** _____ , developed the ten categories for cloud **13)** _____ that are still used today. He divided the clouds into three basic **14)** _____ : Stratus (meaning *stretched out* in Latin), Cumulus (meaning *heap* or *pile*) and Cirrus (*wispy*).

Stratus clouds are low altitude, flat, dull grey coloured and dense. They cover most of the sky and **15)** _____ direct sunlight. Cumulus clouds are middle **16)** _____ , white, puffy and flat at their base. On a warm, sunny day they appear to boil as huge **17)** _____ of heated air rise into the sky. They are formed by water droplets, not ice crystals, which gives them their fluffy **18)** _____ .

Cirrus clouds are high altitude, **19)** _____ and feathery, with tails that curl in the wind. Because they are formed at a higher altitude, the water droplets freeze into millions of tiny ice **20)** _____ .

Cloze Test 27

Select the correct words to complete the passage below.

It was too much. The **1)** [ ] united / [ ] power / [ ] high force of truth and slander and insult put over

heavy a strain on Tom Yorkfield's powers of **2)** [ ] reasons / [ ] restraint / [ ] recall . In his right hand he

held a useful oak **3)** [ ] paddles / [ ] caskets / [ ] cudgel , with his left he made a grab at the **4)** [ ] loose / [ ] limply / [ ] lucid

collar of Laurence's canary-coloured silk shirt. Laurence was not a fighting man; the

fear of **5)** [ ] physical / [ ] gentle / [ ] growing violence threw him off his balance as completely as

overmastering **6)** [ ] poverty / [ ] hunger / [ ] indignation had thrown Tom off his, and thus it came to pass

that Clover Fairy was **7)** [ ] regaled / [ ] content / [ ] regarded with the **8)** [ ] beautiful / [ ] uneventful / [ ] unprecedented sight of a

human being scudding and **9)** [ ] squawking / [ ] laughing / [ ] coughing across the enclosure, like the hen that

would **10)** [ ] die / [ ] desist / [ ] persist in trying to establish a nesting-place in the manger.

Extract from *Sredni Vashtar* by Saki (HH Munro) (1870-1916).

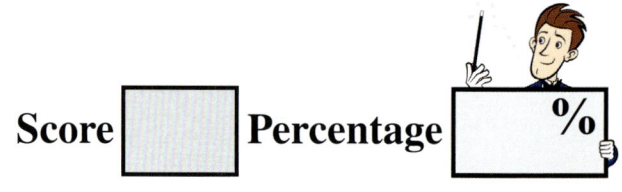

Score [ ] Percentage [ ] %

Cloze Test 28

Fill in the missing letters to complete the passage below.

Alan Mathison Turing was born in Paddington, London in 1912. The headmistress of the day school he first attended 1) `r e _ o _ n i s _ d` his talent early on, as did many of his 2) `s _ b s e _ u e n _` educators and, at the age of 13, he went on to Sherborne School. Turing studied as an 3) `_ n d e r _ r a d _ a t _` from 1931 to 1934 at King's College, Cambridge, from where he gained first-class honours in mathematics. During the Second World War, Turing was a leading 4) `p a _ t _ c i p _ n t` in the breaking of German ciphers at Bletchley Park. He 5) `c o n _ e n _ _ a t e _` on cryptanalysis of the Enigma, with Dilly Knox, a senior codebreaker. Turing had something of a reputation for 6) `_ c c e n t _ i _ i t y` at Bletchley Park. He was known to his 7) `c o _ l e a g _ _ s` as 'Prof' and his 8) `t _ e a t i _ e` on Enigma was known as 'The Prof's Book'. After the war, he worked at the National Physical Laboratory, where he designed the ACE, among the first designs for a stored-program computer. Turing, who was a 9) `_ a l _ n t e _` long-distance runner, 10) `_ c c a s _ o n _ l l _` ran the 40 miles to London when he was needed for high-level meetings. In 1945, Turing was awarded the OBE by King George VI for his wartime services.

Cloze Test 29

Choose the correct words from the word bank below to complete the passage.

furnace	art	dread	sinews	distant
burning	chain	immortal	heart	aspire
anvil	symmetry	clasp	smile	fire
thee	threw	dare	seize	heaven

Tyger! Tyger! **1)** _____ bright

In the forests of the night

What **2)** _____ hand or eye

Could frame thy fearful **3)** _____ ?

In what **4)** _____ deeps or skies

Burnt the **5)** _____ of thine eyes?

On what wings dare he **6)** _____ ?

What the hand, dare **7)** _____ the fire?

And what shoulder, and what **8)** _____ ,

Could twist the **9)** _____ of thy heart?

And when thy **10)** _____ began to beat,

What dread hand? and what **11)** _____ feet?

What the hammer? what the **12)** _____ ?

In what **13)** _____ was thy brain?

What the **14)** _____ ? what dread grasp

Dare its deadly terrors **15)** _____ ?

When the stars **16)** _____ down their spears,

And water'd **17)** _____ with their tears,

Did he **18)** _____ his work to see?

Did he who made the Lamb make **19)** _____ ?

Tyger! Tyger! burning bright

In the forests of the night,

What immortal hand or eye

20) _____ frame thy fearful symmetry?

The Tyger by William Blake (1757–1827).

Cloze Test 30

Fill in the missing letters to complete the passage below.

Grace Darling was born on 24th November 1815 in the town of Bamburgh in Northumberland. Her father, William, was the **1)** k e e _ e _ of the Longstone lighthouse to warn shipping away from the Farne Islands and the **2)** n _ t o r _ o _ s ships' graveyard.

On the night of 7th September 1838, Grace was 22 and living in the lighthouse with her parents. A **3)** s _ v e _ e storm hit the Farne Islands and huge waves were crashing against the lighthouse walls. At **4)** d _ _ b r _ a k the wreck of the paddle steamer Forfarshire could just be seen but when it was fully light survivors could be seen **5)** _ l i _ g i n _ to the fore part of the wreck on Big Harcar Rock. This was all that remained of the ship that had been torn apart by the storm's **6)** f _ r _ c i _ y .

It was impossible for the Sunderland lifeboat on the mainland to launch a rescue attempt in the **7)** a t _ o c _ o _ s conditions. Even Grace's father had doubts about any hope of rescuing the survivors. In spite of this, he and his daughter set out in their 21ft coble to go to their **8)** _ i d . They rowed over a mile through heavy seas, avoiding the rocky islands and **9)** o _ t c r _ p _ completing the **10)** h a _ a r _ o u _ mission twice to rescue nine survivors.

Score [ ] Percentage [ ]%

Cloze Test 31

Fill in the missing letters to complete the passage below.

Tom was somewhat inclined to resent the 1) **patronizing** air of his new friend, a boy of just about his own height and age, but gifted with the most 2) **transcendent** coolness and 3) **assurance**, which Tom felt to be 4) **aggravating** and hard to bear, but couldn't for the life of him help 5) **admiring** and envying—especially when young my lord begins 6) **hectoring** two or three long loafing fellows, half porter, half stableman, with a strong touch of the blackguard, and in the end 7) **arranges** with one of them, 8) **nickname** Cooey, to carry Tom's luggage up to the School-house for sixpence.

"And hark 'ee, Cooey; it must be up in ten minutes, or no more jobs from me. Come along, Brown." And away 9) **swaggered** the young potentate, with his hands in his pockets, and Tom at his side.

"All right, sir," says Cooey, touching his hat, with a leer and a wink at his 10) **companions**.

Extract from *Tom Brown's Schooldays* by Thomas Hughes (1822-1896).

Score ☐ Percentage ☐ %

Cloze Test 32

Select the correct words to complete the passage below.

Captain Robert Falcon Scott, CVO, RN was born in 1868. There were 1) [ ] naval / [ ] tested / [ ] novel

and military 2) [ ] generals / [ ] traditions / [ ] weapons in the family and Scott, aged 13, began his naval

career in 1881 as a cadet. In July 1883, he passed out as a midshipman and

3) [ ] met / [ ] drew / [ ] joined *HMS Boadicea*, the first of several ships on which he served during

his midshipman years. He had 4) [ ] risen / [ ] aspired / [ ] sunk to the rank of lieutenant when, early in

June 1899, while home on leave, he 5) [ ] dreamed / [ ] thought / [ ] learned of an 6) [ ] impending / [ ] excited / [ ] improbable

Antarctic expedition with the *Discovery*, under the 7) [ ] auspices / [ ] named / [ ] flags of the Royal

Geographical Society. Seizing the 8) [ ] moment / [ ] prize / [ ] opportunity for an early command and a

chance to 9) [ ] distinguish / [ ] ingratiate / [ ] absolve himself, Scott volunteered to lead the expedition. The

first expedition had both scientific and exploration 10) [ ] reasons / [ ] objectives / [ ] wishes ; the latter

included a long journey south where Scott set a new southern record by

11) ☐ marching / ☐ run / ☐ skated to latitude 82°S and discovered the Polar Plateau, on which the South Pole is 12) ☐ placed / ☐ based / ☐ located . During the second 13) ☐ vestige / ☐ venture / ☐ outing , Scott led a party of five which reached the South Pole on 17th January 1912, only to find that they had been 14) ☐ preceded / ☐ seen / ☐ captured by Roald Amundsen's Norwegian expedition. On their return journey, Scott's party discovered plant 15) ☐ leaves / ☐ extracts / ☐ fossils , proving Antarctica was once 16) ☐ forested / ☐ hot / ☐ occupied and joined to other continents. At a distance of 150 miles from their base camp and 11 miles from the next 17) ☐ road / ☐ stage / ☐ depot , Scott and his companions died from a combination of 18) ☐ exhaustion / ☐ excitement / ☐ loneliness , starvation and extreme cold. The bodies of Scott and his 19) ☐ wife / ☐ commandes / ☐ companions were discovered by a search party on 12th November 1912 and their records 20) ☐ retrieved / ☐ lost / ☐ burnt . Their final camp became their tomb.

Score ☐   **Percentage** ☐ %

Cloze Test 33

Fill in the missing letters to complete the passage below.

The most **1)** a_s_o_b_i__g thing, however, was the preparations to be made before Colin could be **2)** _ran_port_d with sufficient secrecy to the garden. No one must see the chair-carriage and Dickon and Mary after they turned a certain corner of the **3)** s_ru__ber_ and entered upon the walk outside the ivied walls. As each day passed, Colin had become more and more fixed in his feeling that the **4)** _y_ter_ surrounding the garden was one of its greatest **5)** cha_m_. Nothing must spoil that. No one must ever **6)** _us_e_t that they had a secret. People must think that he was simply going out with Mary and Dickon because he liked them and did not object to their looking at him. They had long and quite **7)** de_i_ht_ul talks about their route. They would go up this path and down that one and cross the other and go round among the **8)** _ou_ta_n flower-beds as if they were looking at the "bedding-out plants" the head gardener, Mr. Roach, had been having arranged. That would seem such a **9)** r_ti_n_l thing to do that no one would think it at all mysterious. They would turn into the shrubbery walks and lose themselves until they came to the long walls. It was almost as serious and **10)** ela_ora_e_y thought out as the plans of march made by great generals in time of war.

Extract from *The Secret Garden* by Frances Hodgson Burnett (1849-1924).

Cloze Test 34

Choose the correct words from the word bank below to complete the passage.

| jar | sprang | gorgeous | flooding | murmuring |
| amazement | dismally | luscious | plumage | awakened |

She was **1)** _____ by a shock, so sudden and severe that if Dorothy had not been lying on the soft bed she might have been hurt. As it was, the **2)** _____ made her catch her breath and wonder what had happened; and Toto put his cold little nose into her face and whined **3)** _____ . Dorothy sat up and noticed that the house was not moving; nor was it dark, for the bright sunshine came in at the window, **4)** _____ the little room. She **5)** _____ from her bed and with Toto at her heels ran and opened the door.

The little girl gave a cry of **6)** _____ and looked about her, her eyes growing bigger and bigger at the wonderful sights she saw.

The cyclone had set the house down very gently - for a cyclone - in the midst of a country of marvelous beauty. There were lovely patches of greensward all about, with stately trees bearing rich and **7)** _____ fruits. Banks of **8)** _____ flowers were on every hand, and birds with rare and brilliant **9)** _____ sang and fluttered in the trees and bushes. A little way off was a small brook, rushing and sparkling along between green banks, and **10)** _____ in a voice very grateful to a little girl who had lived so long on the dry, grey prairies.

Extract from *The Wonderful Wizard of Oz* by L Frank Baum (1856-1919).

Cloze Test 35

Select the correct words to complete the passage below.

Between 1455 and 1487, the **1)** ☐ brief ☐ foreign ☐ dynastic Wars of the Roses were fought in a series of **2)** ☐ sporadic ☐ continuous ☐ compelling episodes. The throne of England was in **3)** ☐ London ☐ turmoil ☐ contention between the supporters of two **4)** ☐ equal ☐ rival ☐ victorious branches of the House of Plantagenet: the houses of York and Lancaster. The **5)** ☐ original ☐ last ☐ preceding Hundred Years' War was a series of conflicts **6)** ☐ waged ☐ wrestled ☐ raged from 1337 to 1453 between the House of Plantagenet, **7)** ☐ ancestors ☐ descendents ☐ rulers of the Kingdom of England, against the House of Valois for **8)** ☐ control ☐ extention ☐ riches of the Kingdom of France. That war left many social and financial **9)** ☐ accounts ☐ benefits ☐ problems for the House of Plantagenet. A further **10)** ☐ contributing ☐ combining ☐ controlling factor was the rise of interest in the rival claim to the throne of Richard, Duke of York, due the mental infirmity and weak rule of the Plantagenet King Henry VI. The **11)** ☐ final ☐ lamentable ☐ latter victory went to a Lancastrian

48 © 2015 Stephen Curran

12) ☐ claimant / ☐ conscript / ☐ consort , Henry Tudor, who defeated the last Yorkist king, Richard III, at the Battle of Bosworth Field. The name Wars of the Roses refers to the Heraldic badges 13) ☐ decorated / ☐ assigned / ☐ associated with the two royal houses: the White Rose of York and the Red Rose of Lancaster. The Yorkist 14) ☐ faction / ☐ women / ☐ towns used the symbol of the white rose from early in the 15) ☐ year / ☐ confines / ☐ conflict but the Lancastrian red rose was only 16) ☐ replaced / ☐ restored / ☐ introduced after Henry's victory. After hostilities 17) ☐ began / ☐ ceased / ☐ erupted , to symbolise the 18) ☐ colours / ☐ wealth / ☐ union of the two houses, the red was 19) ☐ combined / ☐ painted / ☐ entwined with the white rose to form the Tudor Rose. After 20) ☐ losing / ☐ mounting / ☐ assuming the throne as Henry VII, Henry Tudor married Elizabeth of York, the daughter of Edward IV, thereby uniting the two houses. In an era leading to what is sometimes referred to as the "Golden Age" of Elizabeth, the House of Tudor ruled England and Wales until 1603.

Score ☐ Percentage ☐ %

Cloze Test 36

Choose the correct words from the word bank below to complete the passage.

| drapery | secretly | hardened | drapers | discovered |
| dissatisfied | sequins | knack | determined | advertisements |

When there were no visitors, Paul now took his meals with his parents, as he was beyond the nursery control. His mother went into town nearly every day. She had **1)** _____ that she had an odd **2)** _____ of sketching furs and dress materials, so she worked **3)** _____ in the studio of a friend who was the chief 'artist' for the leading **4)** _____ . She drew the figures of ladies in furs and ladies in silk and **5)** _____ for the newspaper **6)** _____ . This young woman artist earned several thousand pounds a year, but Paul's mother only made several hundreds, and she was again **7)** _____ . She so wanted to be first in something, and she did not succeed, even in making sketches for **8)** _____ advertisements.

She was down to breakfast on the morning of her birthday. Paul watched her face as she read her letters. He knew the lawyer's letter. As his mother read it, her face **9)** _____ and became more expressionless. Then a cold, **10)** _____ look came on her mouth. She hid the letter under the pile of others, and said not a word about it.

"Didn't you have anything nice in the post for your birthday, mother?" said Paul.

"Quite moderately nice," she said, her voice cold and hard and absent.

Extract from *The Rocking Horse Winner* by DH Lawrence (1885-1930).

Cloze Test 37

Fill in the missing letters to complete the passage below.

A Robin said: The Spring will never come,

And I shall never care to build again.

A Rosebush said: These frosts are 1) wearisome,

My sap will never 2) stir for sun or rain.

The half Moon said: These nights are 3) foggiest and slow,

I neither care to wax nor care to wane.

The Ocean said: I 4) thirst from long ago,

Because earth's 5) rivers cannot fill the main. —

When 6) Springtime came, red Robin built a nest,

And 7) trilled a lover's song in sheer delight.

Grey 8) hoarfrost vanished, and the Rose with might

Clothed her in leaves and buds of crimson core.

The dim Moon 9) brightened. Ocean sunned his crest,

Dimpled his blue, yet 10) thirsted evermore.

A Wintry Sonnet by Christina Rossetti (1830-1894).

Cloze Test 38

Choose the correct words from the word bank below to complete the passage.

former	compromised	secured	aristocratic	campaigns
spanned	branch	regarded	opposition	retiring
ranking	assemblies	gaining	influential	steadfastly
honour	returned	inspire	election	entrance

Sir Winston Leonard Spencer-Churchill was born in 1874 into the 1) _____ family of the Dukes of Marlborough, a 2) _____ of the Spencer family. He was educated at Harrow and, on leaving in 1893, he applied to join the Royal Military College at Sandhurst. He passed the 3) _____ exam at his third attempt and, because the grade required to join the cavalry was lower rather than for the infantry, he applied for the 4) _____ . Training for the cavalry also lacked the requirement to learn mathematics, which Churchill disliked. He saw action in India, the Sudan and the second Boer War, 5) _____ fame as a war correspondent for the *Morning Post* and writing books about his 6) _____ .

He resigned from the army and in the general election of 1900 he was 7) _____ to parliament as the Conservative member for Oldham. So began his long political career which 8) _____ fifty years.

During the Second World War, following the resignation of Neville Chamberlain in May 1940, Churchill became Prime Minister. He 9) _____ refused to consider defeat, surrender, or a 10) _____ peace during the difficult early days of the war when the British Commonwealth and Empire stood alone in its active

11) _____ to Adolf Hitler. Churchill's speeches and radio broadcasts helped 12) _____ the British people. He led Britain as Prime Minister until victory over Nazi Germany had been 13) _____ .

The Conservative Party lost the 1945 general 14) _____ and Churchill became Leader of the Opposition to the Labour Government. After winning the 1951 election, he again became Prime Minister, before 15) _____ in 1955.

Upon his death, Queen Elizabeth II granted him the 16) _____ of a state funeral, which saw one of the largest 17) _____ of world statesmen in history. Named the Greatest Briton of all time in a 2002 poll, Churchill is widely 18) _____ as being among the most 19) _____ people in British history, consistently 20) _____ well in opinion polls of Prime Ministers of the United Kingdom.

Cloze Test 39

Select the correct words to complete the passage below.

As early as the fifth century BC, Socrates is quoted: "If we hadn't a voice or a

1) [ ] song / [ ] tongue / [ ] nose , and wanted to 2) [ ] express / [ ] expel / [ ] donate things to one another, wouldn't we

try to make signs by 3) [ ] wringing / [ ] moving / [ ] waving our hands, head, and the rest of our body, just

as 4) [ ] blind / [ ] dumb / [ ] old people do at present?" For centuries 5) [ ] doctors / [ ] sailors / [ ] communities have used

sign language, or signing, to communicate between deaf people. It is also used

by those who can hear 6) [ ] perfectly / [ ] poorly / [ ] sounds but are unable to 7) [ ] eat / [ ] say / [ ] speak . There are

many 8) [ ] variations / [ ] variety / [ ] version of sign language used around the world and, like a spoken

language, they all differ but may have certain 9) [ ] strange / [ ] useful / [ ] fundamental properties that

exist in all languages. It is interesting to 10) [ ] note / [ ] notice / [ ] know that two countries that share

a common 11) [ ] foreign / [ ] spoken / [ ] English language may find the other's sign language completely

12) [ ] uninteresting / [ ] unbelievable / [ ] unintelligible . For example, American Sign Language is quite different

from the British **13)** ☐ preference / ☐ equivalent / ☐ perspective. Signing not only employs the use of hands and fingers; non-manual movements of other parts of the **14)** ☐ anatomy / ☐ bodies / ☐ torso, such as head, cheeks, eyebrows and mouth may also be used to **15)** ☐ concoct / ☐ control / ☐ convey information.

It is also interesting that **16)** ☐ language / ☐ discourse / ☐ play involving one or more persons signing is **17)** ☐ prevented / ☐ encourage / ☐ structured through the use of eye gaze and head movement. The signer has to be watched by others **18)** ☐ engaged / ☐ mentioned / ☐ enthralled in conversation and is thus able to **19)** ☐ avast / ☐ scribe / ☐ avoid the others 'speaking' by not **20)** ☐ looking / ☐ shouting / ☐ pointing at them.

Score ☐   **Percentage** ☐ %

Cloze Test 40

Choose the correct words from the word bank below to complete the passage.

destroyed	**invaders**	**ruler**	**capital**	**augmented**
imposition	**defeated**	**rebellion**	**resented**	**confiscated**

She is often referred to as Boudicea but her correct name is Boudica. The name Boudica means 'Victoria' and, in AD 43, she led the native Britons in a 1) _____ against the Roman 2) _____ who had ruled southern Briton for seventeen years.

She was married to Prasutagus, the 3) _____ of the Iceni people. After the invasion, he was allowed by the Romans to continue as king and rule the Iceni people on their behalf.

On the death of Prasutagus, the Romans 4) _____ the property of the leading Iceni families and imposed their rule on the people directly. The Britons 5) _____ the Romans and the 6) _____ of direct Roman rule prompted Boudica to lead a revolt.

Her warrior army, 7) _____ by other tribes who joined her, defeated one Roman army. They also 8) _____ Colchester, which was then the 9) _____ of Roman Britain, London and Verulamium (the Roman name for St. Albans). Boudica was finally 10) _____ by the Romans after fierce battles where many Britons were killed. It is believed that Boudica took her own life with poison.

Answers

11+ Verbal Activity
Year 5-7 Cloze Testbook 1

Test 1
1) shaking
2) running
3) denied
4) windy
5) flung
6) spume
7) vagrant
8) whetted
9) laughing
10) sweet

Test 2
1) admitted
2) rebellion
3) buckled
4) served
5) effective
6) boosted
7) promoted
8) referred
9) decisive
10) campaign
11) surrendered
12) dispatched
13) coalition
14) Unfortunately
15) defeat
16) overshadowed
17) fame
18) exemplary
19) sacrificed
20) advance

Test 3
1) massive
2) mighty
3) horror
4) recorded
5) dropped
6) slacked
7) motors
8) burning
9) smoke
10) screaming

Test 4
1) launched
2) transmitter
3) successful
4) propaganda
5) demonstrated
6) initially
7) progress
8) heralded
9) narrative
10) protests

Test 5
1) conceived
2) morale
3) ceased
4) homeless
5) attacked
6) bombardment
7) accommodate
8) issued
9) responsible
10) withstand
11) sirens
12) descended
13) explosive
14) entrances
15) sheltering
16) provide
17) navigate
18) incendiary
19) marker
20) avoiding

Test 6
1) issued
2) reconcile
3) rebel
4) swift
5) payments
6) liberty
7) cited
8) constitutional
9) foundation
10) arbitrary

Test 7
1) singing
2) vista
3) tingling
4) poised
5) insidious
6) Betrays
7) tinkling
8) glamour
9) manhood
10) remembrance

Test 8
1) Russian
2) basket
3) hemmed
4) frightened
5) whenever
6) several
7) whereabouts
8) strange
9) Parliament
10) corrected
11) kindly
12) constantly
13) hyena
14) surrounded
15) clover

© 2015 Stephen Curran

11+ Verbal Activity
Year 5-7 Cloze Testbook 1

Answers

16) beckoned
17) concealed
18) promising
19) recollect
20) ripe

Test 9
1) née
2) engrossed
3) diet
4) degree
5) element
6) native
7) radioactive
8) coined
9) receive
10) illness

Test 10
1) invented
2) casting
3) press
4) composition
5) profession
6) comprising
7) low
8) economical
9) composed
10) characters

Test 11
1) depression
2) Subsequent
3) compresses
4) trapped
5) expelled
6) overflows
7) weakness
8) terrain
9) combine

10) abrades
11) typically
12) increases
13) lateral
14) width
15) Vast
16) reservoir
17) exception
18) temperatures
19) otherwise
20) lacking

Test 12
1) experience
2) squealing
3) huge
4) arched
5) caravans
6) tethered
7) drawing
8) creaking
9) cuffing
10) packed

Test 13
1) energy
2) decayed
3) occurring
4) relatively
5) poorer
6) Formation
7) primarily
8) sedimentary
9) compressed
10) rank

Test 14
1) beneath
2) Lingering
3) evening

4) nestle
5) Eager
6) simple
7) paled
8) Echoes
9) slain
10) haunts
11) moving
12) waking
13) tale
14) willing
15) Lovingly
16) Dreaming
17) summers
18) drifting
19) golden
20) dream

Test 15
1) order
2) species
3) majority
4) creatures
5) shelter
6) varieties
7) figure
8) sensory
9) iridescent
10) naked

Test 16
1) feathers
2) perches
3) without
4) sweetest
5) storm
6) abash
7) chillest
8) strangest

Answers

11+ Verbal Activity
Year 5-7 Cloze Testbook 1

9) Extremity
10) crumb

Test 17
1) speaking
2) glazed
3) gazing
4) description
5) vaults
6) horrid
7) decay
8) dusty
9) crooked
10) tightly
11) inaudible
12) stir
13) awoke
14) boarded
15) courage
16) common
17) ascertain
18) impressed
19) muslin
20) confided

Test 18
1) system
2) engineering
3) flights
4) vessel
5) opposite
6) massive
7) embedded
8) lake
9) enormous
10) heaviest

Test 19
1) novelist
2) brought

3) numerous
4) classic
5) animated
6) awarded
7) recipient
8) declined
9) appointment
10) success

Test 20
1) settled
2) conclude
3) genetic
4) inhabitants
5) Inca
6) comprised
7) indigenous
8) illustrations
9) trunks
10) hemp
11) lashed
12) plaited
13) thatched
14) blade
15) dimensions
16) crewed
17) companions
18) smashed
19) landfall
20) display

Test 21
1) commenced
2) terminating
3) probably
4) vary
5) dominant
6) posed
7) advantages
8) ensuing

9) insurrection
10) enthusiastic

Test 22
1) Evidence
2) practising
3) preserved
4) value
5) vessels
6) react
7) coagulate
8) agitation
9) objective
10) batch

Test 23
1) traces
2) cautious
3) mincing
4) dubiously
5) ingratiating
6) menacing
7) retreated
8) corresponding
9) luring
10) vague
11) dissipated
12) sniffed
13) coy
14) rifle
15) sled
16) mistake
17) bounding
18) snarl
19) regaining
20) holding

Test 24
1) dependent
2) determined

11+ Verbal Activity
Year 5-7 Cloze Testbook 1

Answers

3) materials
4) predominantly
5) protection
6) stalked
7) dominating
8) ultimately
9) campaign
10) strategic

Test 25
1) attended
2) declined
3) acquired
4) missions
5) named
6) confirmed
7) rift
8) convicted
9) exile
10) brutally

Test 26
1) cycle
2) atmosphere
3) gas
4) condensed
5) droplets
6) Eventually
7) precipitation
8) hail
9) process
10) endless
11) varies
12) meteorologist
13) identification
14) shapes
15) obscure
16) altitude
17) bubbles
18) appearance
19) wispy
20) crystals

Test 27
1) united
2) restraint
3) cudgel
4) loose
5) physical
6) indignation
7) regaled
8) unprecedented
9) squawking
10) persist

Test 28
1) recognised
2) subsequent
3) undergraduate
4) participant
5) concentrated
6) eccentricity
7) colleagues
8) treatise
9) talented
10) occasionally

Test 29
1) burning
2) immortal
3) symmetry
4) distant
5) fire
6) aspire
7) seize
8) art
9) sinews
10) heart
11) dread
12) chain
13) furnace
14) anvil
15) clasp
16) threw
17) heaven
18) smile
19) thee
20) dare

Test 30
1) keeper
2) notorious
3) severe
4) daybreak
5) clinging
6) ferocity
7) atrocious
8) aid
9) outcrops
10) hazardous

Test 31
1) patronizing
2) transcendent
3) assurance
4) aggravating
5) admiring
6) hectoring
7) arranges
8) nicknamed
9) swaggers
10) companions

Test 32
1) naval
2) traditions
3) joined
4) risen
5) learned
6) impending

Answers

11+ Verbal Activity
Year 5-7 Cloze Testbook 1

7) auspices
8) opportunity
9) distinguish
10) objectives
11) marching
12) located
13) venture
14) preceded
15) fossils
16) forested
17) depot
18) exhaustion
19) companions
20) retrieved

Test 33
1) absorbing
2) transported
3) shrubbery
4) mystery
5) charms
6) suspect
7) delightful
8) fountain
9) rational
10) elaborately

Test 34
1) awakened
2) jar
3) dismally
4) flooding
5) sprang
6) amazement
7) luscious
8) gorgeous
9) plumage
10) murmuring

Test 35
1) dynastic
2) sporadic
3) contention
4) rival
5) preceding
6) waged
7) rulers
8) control
9) problems
10) contributing
11) final
12) claimant
13) associated
14) faction
15) conflict
16) introduced
17) ceased
18) union
19) combined
20) assuming

Test 36
1) discovered
2) knack
3) secretly
4) drapers
5) sequins
6) advertisements
7) dissatisfied
8) drapery
9) hardened
10) determined

Test 37
1) wearisome
2) stir
3) fogged
4) thirst
5) rivers
6) Springtime
7) trilled
8) hoarfrost
9) brightened
10) thirsted

Test 38
1) aristocratic
2) branch
3) entrance
4) former
5) gaining
6) campaigns
7) returned
8) spanned
9) steadfastly
10) compromised
11) opposition
12) inspire
13) secured
14) election
15) retiring
16) honour
17) assemblies
18) regarded
19) influential
20) ranking

Test 39
1) tongue
2) express
3) moving
4) dumb
5) communities
6) perfectly
7) speak
8) variations
9) fundamental
10) note
11) spoken

11+ Verbal Activity
Year 5-7 Cloze Testbook 1

Answers

12) unintelligible
13) equivalent
14) anatomy
15) convey
16) discourse
17) structured
18) engaged
19) avoid
20) looking

Test 40
1) rebellion
2) invaders
3) ruler
4) confiscated
5) resented
6) imposition
7) augmented
8) destroyed
9) capital
10) defeated

PROGRESS CHARTS

Test	Mark	%	Test	Mark	%
1			21		
2			22		
3			23		
4			24		
5			25		
6			26		
7			27		
8			28		
9			29		
10			30		
11			31		
12			32		
13			33		
14			34		
15			35		
16			36		
17			37		
18			38		
19			38		
20			40		

Overall Percentage | **%**

CERTIFICATE OF

ACHIEVEMENT

This certifies

_____

has successfully completed

11+ Verbal Activity
Year 5–7 Cloze
TESTBOOK 1

Overall percentage score achieved [ ] %

Comment _____

_____

Signed _____
(teacher/parent/guardian)

Date _____